The Fiddler of Driskill Hill

THE FIDDLER OF DRISKILL HILL

POEMS

David Middleton

Louisiana State University Press

Baton Rouge

Published with the assistance of the Sea Cliff Fund

Published by Louisiana State University Press
Copyright © 2013 by David Middleton
All rights reserved
Manufactured in the United States of America
LSU Press Paperback Original
First printing

Designer: Emily Sarah Manuel
Typefaces: display, Old Claude; text, Adobe Garamond Pro
Printer and binder: McNaughton & Gunn

Library of Congress Cataloging-in-Publication Data
Middleton, David, 1949–
  [Poems. Selections]
  The fiddler of Driskill Hill : poems / David Middleton.
     pages cm
  "LSU Press Paperback Original"—T.p. verso.
  ISBN 978-0-8071-5196-9 (paper : alk. paper) — ISBN 978-0-8071-5197-6 (pdf) — ISBN 978-0-8071-5198-3 (epub) — ISBN 978-0-8071-5199-0 (mobi)
  I. Title.
  PS3563.I362F53 2014
  811'.54—dc23

                                                              2012048401

The paper in this book meets the guidelines for permanence and durability of the Committee on Production Guidelines for Book Longevity of the Council on Library Resources. ∞

A number of these poems appeared—sometimes in slightly different form—in the chapbooks *As Far As Light Remains* (The Cummington Press, 1993), *Bonfires on the Levee* (Blue Heron Press, 1996), *The Undivided Realm* (Robert L. Barth Press, 2000), and *The Language of the Heart* (Louisiana Literature Chapbook Series, Chapbook 4, Louisiana Literature Press, 2003), and in the anthologies *Points of Gold: Poems for Leo Luke Marcello*, edited with an introduction by Stella Ann Nesanovich, (Xavier Review Press, 2005) and in *2012 Jambalaya Writers' Conference Anthology* (Terrebonne Parish Library, 2013), edited by Daryl Holmes.

Also, the author wishes to thank the editors of the following journals for publishing many of the poems herein collected: *The Anglican: A Journal of Anglican Identity; The Anglican Theological Review; Arator: A Journal of Southern History, Thought and Culture; Chronicles: A Magazine of American Culture; Critical Quarterly; Desire Street; Drastic Measures; The Epigrammatist; First Things; The Formalist; Image: A Journal of the Arts and Religion; The Louisiana English Journal; Louisiana Literature; The Louisiana Review; The Lyric; Modern Age; POEM; The Sewanee Review; Smartish Pace;* and *The Southern Review.*

*in memory of George Garrett (1929–2008),
man of letters, poet, friend of poets*

and

*Wilmer Mills (1969–2011),
Louisiana poet whose words and music sing us back to Eden*

and for

*Lindon Stall,
lifelong friend and fellow poet,*
Et in Arcadia ego

Throw out the radio and take down the fiddle from the wall.

—*Andrew Lytle, "The Hind Tit,"* I'll Take My Stand (1930)

✼

"Old Louisiana" [1877–1920] . . .
a leisurely time when no one was in too much of a hurry. . . .
They still retained most of their old customs and living habits. . . .
There were no funeral homes then. Everyone was buried from his own home. . . .
The home, throughout the period, was the center of life.

—*Edwin Adams Davis,* Louisiana: The Pelican State (1975)

✼

If you plow on Good Friday the lightning will strike your field,
and the ground will bleed.

—*Lyle Saxon, "Superstitions,"* Old Louisiana (1929)

✼

After Louisiana nothing seemed real.

—*Robert Penn Warren,* in *Thomas W. Cutrer,* Parnassus on the Mississippi:
The Southern Review and the Baton Rouge Literary Community, 1935–1942
(1984)

Contents

Bonfires on the Levee	1
Winter into Spring	3
In Waking Dream	4
The Breakers	7
North Louisiana Country Church in Flames	8
The Singing Wires	10
The Deep End	11
Hand-Me-Downs	12
Leaving Drexel Street: A Wife's Goodbye	13
Summer Ending	15
In Allen Hall	16
Upon the Publication of a First Book of Poems	18
Warren in Thibodaux	19
Rapture at Twilight	20
Janitor	21
The Courtyard Plum	22
Before and After Reading	23
The Fairfield Gnomes	24
Daddy	25
Mother among the Graves	28
Deep Country Epitaph	29
Two for Life	31
In Winter Prime	32

Black Lake Tales	33
Flies and Grounders	39
In the Bleak Midwinter	41
"If I should die before I wake": Of a Daughter Who Died at the Age of Ten	43
The Latchkey Child	45
Home	50
The Farmer's Almanac	51
The Sniper: Last Report from a Louisianian in Lee's Tigers	53
Song of the Overseer	56
The Reenactor	57
The Given World	58
Epiphany in Lent	64
Parishioners	65
White Wings: Of Kate Mulvaney, Irish Acadian Traiteur	67
After Katrina: Noah's Raven	71
Hurricane Baby	73
The Fiddler of Driskill Hill	74

The Fiddler of Driskill Hill

Bonfires on the Levee

for Burt Cestia

Late autumn days we labor in the swamps
Or by the river bank's entangled brush
Gathering cane and willow wood to dry,
Then cut and stack and soak in kerosene—
Towers showing the way to Papa Noël
Riding over the beaches and the bluffs—
Lining the River Road near Baton Rouge
Where north Louisiana yields at last,
Though stubbornly, to customs of the south
White cotton bolls becoming sweet green cane
And the Mississippi, ready for the Gulf,
Foaming in salt beyond the salted marsh.

Then when Christmas Eve recedes into a night
So distant from the shepherds and the Star,
We torch the settled base-logs one by one
Watching fires rise more like the beaconed peaks
That spread from Troy to Thrace and Thessaly
Than candles of the body and the blood.
Unchristened constellations made to blaze
Beyond the last millennium's passing end—
The stars' coeval gleamings in the dark
Appear as faintest signals from a source
Whose love would touch each bonfire's sparkling bark
Even in this remotest holy post.

And by such light we glimpse what sense commends
In this strange state subsiding like our lives
From foothills of the Ozarks rippling out
In gardens of the strong-stemmed Shreveport rose
Down through the dense Kisatchie once preserved
By Carrie Dormon's will into the central farms
Of soybeans and corn then further on below
South to the bottomlands whose fallow mold
The wild strawberries redden every spring
And plump mushrooms make white in autumn dawns
Where settlers three short centuries ago
Parted man-high grass and saw the buffalo.

Such are the chief ingredients of our roux—
The mantled sands and gravels, oil and gas
Welling from ancient deltas, rising domes
Pushed up from the mother-bed of primal salt
All thickening this rich gumbo eons stirred—
The fossil olives, laurels, hollies, figs,
Gullies of maidenhair untouched by spring's
Chill sun, late winter's early mallows
Trembling in a telic realm where bears
Coming to fish under a Hunter's Moon
Paw deeply in the streams for goggle-eyes
Or maul dried hives for honey in the noon.

And now as the last charred logs collapse in ash
Blown twinkling in the cindered distances
Over the farther arpents' sunken clays
We give ourselves to what we had possessed
Too rudely in the day, this drained estate
Through which the river straining at its banks
Crests like the fallen waters Noah rode
When Chaos broke again through its black crevasse
Out of the leveed heavens whose bonfires
Like our own declare the drifted silt
Poured off a shelving continent's worn edge
To lie undredged over DeSoto's bones.

Winter into Spring
Thibodaux, Louisiana

We drive north to New Orleans this far south
Where land and sea both lose themselves in marsh
And spring breaks through mild winter's brittle cold
When pansies blaze over the noon-light's ice.
We know, of course, the rare unsparing day
When sovereign Arctic blasts sweep south-southeast
Freezing the boughs of budding fig and pear
As in the fall and summer kindred winds
Bring down from mobile thrones of blade and air
Our ladybug and monarch butterfly.

But these are open winters where the sun
Tempers the sleet to rain and makes a dew
Of snowflakes on the maiden maple leaf.
And even in a January dawn,
Awakened by the salt breath of the Gulf,
Dutch clover, yellow mustard, and a thin
Unbending periwinkle on a stalk
Deep-rooted in its terra-cotta pot
Spread hues and scents across pale frosted lawns
Till once more spring's green regency has come.

In Waking Dream
Nicholls State University, Thibodaux; and Grand Isle, Louisiana

for Alice

Most days I pass your open office door
To find you grading papers, rubber band
Bound sets of awkward adolescent gropings
Toward classic architectures of the soul
Where sentence, clause, and phrase and single words
Build paragraphs that should support the whole.
And with your desk lamp bent toward each white page,
Your pen now poised, now marking faults in red,
You seem the good physician of our tongue
Gazing with your intense yet gentle face
On all those grave contagions of the human
Heart and mind—wrong cases, fragments, run-ons,
Letters and numbers somehow gone astray—
And you would make it better with your mild
And sterner cures, a justified D-minus
Balanced by mercy's note: "Karen, you have
Ability and often write quite well.
Please see me in my office. I can help."

Yet when at times you tire of both diseases
And their physic, you drive down to Grand Isle
Leaving a while the disciplines of speech
To walk the beach at evening as graceful
As a heron but with movements all your own.
And there you stay and look upon the Gulf—
Stars rising in their fires through lakes of space
Out of the ocean's swelling salt and dark,
Storm petrels taking sea trout from the waves,
The wild oats sowing seeds in windy dunes—
And sense in that one place all mystery,
Creation's ancient language no one knows,
That elemental syntax of the world
Still roaring in the seashell and the sea.

And in a year long past my given days
I picture you retired at eighty-five,
Still teaching part-time, walking with a cane

Then indispensable, those Grand Isle nights
In wonder on the beach just memories.
And if I may permit myself to dream
Perhaps you'll make your slow bone-aching way
To my old office down that narrow hall,
A room by some young colleague occupied,
And think of one who wrote about the surf,
Those breakers and the kingdom of the things.
And when at last the past will have its way,
In spite of shortened breath and stiffened knees,
Knowing you have to see Grand Isle once more,
You'll charm that nice young man who had usurped
Unwittingly the office of a poet
And make him drive you down to watch the Gulf
One clearest winter evening (though only
From the window of the car), and you will walk
In spirit on the beach and think of earth
As that grand isle of all the life we know
Worn down by time and space's steady waves.

And if your driver sees warm welling tears
Filling the deepened wrinkles of your cheeks
Perhaps you'll tell him as he looks aside,
"It's nothing, just a few remembered lines,
Some verses someone sent me long ago.
He'd see me grading papers, I suppose,
From what he wrote and left me on my desk.
He was a southern gentleman, standing
Up for ladies still in 1999.
I never guessed he thought of me at all
But poets see right through you when you don't
Even know they're looking. Then you waken
To the world's unending mystery again.
He touched me at a depth no one had touched
That way before. Perhaps I did the same
For him as muse, although he never said.
The poem is lost. I can't recall his face

Except in dream, or now, in waking dream.
I walked these Grand Isle beaches as a girl
And found that words, to which I've pledged my life,
Lay latent in the soundings of the waves.
He knew that much about me. Take me home."

The Breakers
Grand Isle, Louisiana

Late afternoons we walk upon the sand
Where breakers make the world that we desire,
This meeting-place of air and sea and land
Washed from the bright prime element of fire.

Pelicans heading westward with the day,
Shells rolling in surf, the shifting dunes in flower
Never knowing when we come or go away,
These stay within their changes hour by hour.

Near twilight we wade out beneath pale skies
That darken till the stars at eventide
Let flow upon the foam about our thighs
Faint rays from those far homes where they abide.

So noble in their hallowed altitudes
The stars withstand the breakers of the waste,
Lords of the lunar dunes their light includes,
Now braced against the void they once embraced.

And though no cold, remote, untainted mind
Can free us from these nights through which we roam,
The salted blood is stellar, like in kind
To wisdom's salt come shoreward on the foam.

Old Maker, who still binds in tidal rhyme
The rhythms of poiesis and this place,
Your metrics measure heaven where in time
Things burst in holy closures of your grace.

North Louisiana Country Church in Flames
Bienville Parish, the mid-1950s

Late Christmas Eve and now long hours begin
For a boy whose mother's welcome hearthside kiss
Closes old tales of no room at the inn
And leads to dreams of lighted trees and this:

A sleep disturbed by strangely glittering gifts
Waiting under the bubble-candled fir,
Then by a wind that through a cracked pane lifts
Curtains the faint smoke-traces lace and stir.

The child in time awakens, sniffs, and peers
Blearily through the window toward a flame
Climbing far steeple-timbers till his fears
And eyes fix on a church's gleaming frame.

The rest his roused grandfather, whom he'd tell,
Related hours after when the splash
Of dawn-light drenched the still flickering hell
Where tongues unnumbered babbled in the ash.

Stunned deacons first crushed-in the smoldering doors
Meeting a Red Sea blazing in the nave
Uncrossable to reach those Jordan shores
Beyond the scalded baptistry's raised wave.

Then bearing lists of weddings, births, and deaths,
One dashed by the pastor's study and the choir,
Glimpsing the pulpit Bible's dragon breaths,
Its Book of Revelation laved in fire.

The smoke-choked deacons stumbled out for air
As winds took up the holocaust that spread
Under spiked railings' incandescent glare
To lay its pall of flame upon the dead.

And as those gathered watched each cindered grave
Glowing below a stone's seared name and date,
The church's crackling rafters cracked and gave
In to the great cremation uncreate.

That yuletide night no cows or oxen knelt,
No cocks crowed evil spirits well away,
And no one knew what then a child had felt
Walking those charred foundations Christmas Day.

Yet there beside a melted cross and bell
Clutching his gift, a book of tales, the boy
First saw that world in which each man must dwell,
Aeneas bearing Vesta out of Troy.

The Singing Wires
Saline, Bienville Parish, north Louisiana,
December 1960

The Christmas giving over, he strolled in the great mundane,
Sad aftermath to wonder, the same old world again,
A boy not yet twelve but with a man's imagination,
Waiting for the muse's fatal instigation.

And going down the welcome-walk where pink wood sorrel grew
Long summers when he wandered, prince of all he knew,
He smelled no blazoned fragrances from blooms withered and gone
But gazed on high-pitched phone wires, stark and taut in dawn.

The walk led to a gravel drive with pebbles gleaming bright—
Translucent yellow, rust, and pink, gray, black, and cloudy white—
And up above them, some ways off, those telephone wires strung
One line above another, pole to pole, straight hung.

The scene looked like a lined white page or like a music sheet
Designed for sounds of words or notes high above the street.
The boy scooped up a good handful of many-tinted stones
To hit the wires and set off twanging monotones.

He threw sidearm and overhead—rocks jagged, flat, and round—
Some zinging wires that whined with vibrant cadenced sound
Though most stones arced and fell away through silence to the sand
Washed from pinewood slopes to build up watermelon land.

The boy soon tired of what it took to keep the wires singing
And so the lines grew still again although they kept on ringing
Inside the mind of one almost ready to comprehend
The muse had chosen him that day as hers for her own end.

And so in time his lines like wires would thrill with carol, song,
Eclogue, georgic, elegy, and anthem set along
This wold's millennium-rhythms, iambic hills one hears
Measured out in eons like the music of the spheres.

The Deep End
Cedar Grove Pool,
Shreveport, Louisiana, 1955

in memory of my father, David V. Middleton, Jr. (1922–1996)

So tentatively stepping to the end
Of the limber board until my clenching toes
Felt for the edge while counterpoising hands
And a twisting torso sought the balance point,
I stared down at the water where you stayed
Treading slowly, waiting for me to leap
Or dive into the deep end and your arms
One Sunday afternoon when public pools,
Like all the blue-lawed town, were closed all day
Except to you, their summer manager.

I knew my way around the shallow end
Where first I bobbed in inner tubes and then
Went under after pennies on the bright green floor
That sloped down as I floated toward a rope
Beyond which lay the great unwaded dark,
Emerald and unending in the eyes
Of a scared boy standing on the diving board
Hesitant as you yelled for him to jump.

And so, trembling and teetering on the edge,
Wavering between pure trust and total fear
I weakly sprang collapsing in a splash,
Then looked up paddling with my gasps and cries
Toward you who had removed yourself a ways
To make me swim through dead brown water bugs
And sand flies stinging as I rose and sank
Toward where you held your hand out from the bank.

And now for three long years you've swum alone
Breathlessly through death's unfathomed pool
While at your gravestone's marble board I stand
Trembling and looking down to find you there
Treading the darkest depths we'll ever know,
Waters through which my soul must also go
With faith and fear that bore me up before
To clasp a hand extended from the shore.

Hand-Me-Downs

She wheels her chair beside a locked oak chest
That holds both christening and wedding gowns,
Her mother's things she's always cherished best
And worn herself, love's heirloom hand-me-downs.

Her husband far afield pushes a plow
His father made to break this fertile land
That he as father works with his son now,
The well-worn handles passed from hand to hand.

The son's put on his father's overalls,
Just come to manhood and a grownup's size;
A daughter wraps her mother-woven shawls
Across full breasts no shawl or blouse disguise.

This family knows that little's really new,
That most of life's comprised of hand-me-downs
Someone before us thought or made or grew,
Then gave or left us like a mother's gowns

Or Bible with its ever-spreading tree
Whose limbs bear names like those oak limbs outside
Young grandsons calling mount with that same glee
Their grandma felt who wheels to watch them ride.

Leaving Drexel Street
A Wife's Goodbye
August 1990, 942 Drexel Street, Southern Heights,
Shreveport, Louisiana

for my mother, Anna Sudduth Middleton

The sun is going down on our last day
As on the first in this the only house
That we, as man and wife, have ever owned:
Stacked boxes packed and numbered once again,
The wedding service worn with use and love—
Cracked china, tarnished silver—wrapped in sheets
Of *Shreveport Times* whose syndicated reams
Say nothing of this home I kept and made and dreamed.

Outside, the front yard's red-brick flowerbed
Still blooms with portulaca planted there
When these splotched hands were rosy as the heads
That bow and close in latest summer dusk
While I, as my sick husband, sitting, waits
For movers to remove us from our world,
Must walk one final time these rooms I share
With ghosts that speak and breathe in memory's breathless air:

The parlor where we met in formal dress
The pastor, salesman, candidate, new friend;
The dining room where fasting met repast,
Those bowls and greens our kiln and garden gave;
The kitchen whose bright rites of knife and fire
Prepared the table's meat, fish, leaf, and root;
The bathroom where we washed, then drained away
The soil and oil and dust—refuse of all our days;

The bedroom where we lay to gaze and love,
At deepest peace with seasons of the stars,
Where, when our son was born, we snuggled up
To read him lore of Mother Goose and Grimm,
Of Greece and England, Rome and Bethlehem—
Fathering wonders hidden in the words
That call all children home from the absurd,
Great stable tales that lift the bidden heart and mind.

But now the movers come: the dark van waits
To haul off all these recollected things
In one blank clanging chamber to our boy
With whom we now will live in love's last rooms
Near far Acadian marshes well below
This river bluff's crimped hills, these Southern Heights
We'll leave when one more watering is done,
A parting bride's moss roses still touched by setting suns.

Summer Ending

Green blades grow pale and still
Below this windowsill
Whose clearest panes
A sheer light stains,
Then passes where it will.

The grass's crickets cry,
Compelled to mate and die,
And thus to share,
Though unaware,
In my more chilling sigh.

For here I rock and stare,
Grown old in this old chair,
Alert to what
Crickets are not,
Hope woven with despair.

The first leaves reach my door,
Pecan and sycamore,
As summer ends
And fall portends
What winter knows before.

In Allen Hall

Louisiana State University, Baton Rouge, Louisiana

1. Of Textual Editing

text < Lt. *textus, texere*—woven, to weave >

for R. W. Crump

I pass among the stacks in those cool rooms
Where manuscripts stay dry in box and dark,
Papers laid out on shelves like family tombs,
Dated by ink, hand, font, or watermark.

My task is daunting, haunted by defeat,
To guess the last best words an author meant—
Collating each saved draft, each printed sheet,
Blue-penciled proofs—the matter of intent.

And though today loud Humpty Dumptys claim
That words mean only what we *say* they mean,
Yet I in quiet will weigh them just the same,
By Pilate, Cain, and Eden's snake unseen:

For editors of texts have always known
How tentative, unstable words can be—
High tongues of Babel dumbstruck on the stone,
Tragic ash in the Alexandrine sea.

But if we cannot fix by imprimatur
Platonic absolutes, some perfect verse,
Penelope by Homer woven pure,
We still believe in better texts and worse

Unlike those who declare all words absurd,
Corrupted wits unfit to serve a king,
The Word Made Flesh, suffering to be heard,
His life a holograph whose psalm we sing.

2. Near Viareggio

August 16, 1822
il buon tempo verrà

in memory of Annette McCormick

The waves that left him bloated on the shore—
The wet pale skin, the red salt-streaming hair—
Washed yellow toward the shallow grave that bore
Beneath its three spaced stakes what brought them there:

Trelawny, Byron, Hunt, the helpers hired
To dig up flesh white lime stained indigo—
Fish-eaten face and arms now furnace-fired,
Poured wine and oil soaking logs stacked below.

And as his ashes floated high in light
On west winds toward the whitest Apennines
Or when his body died into its night,
Soul overwhelmed by Adonais' lines,

The unlocked Bible, Jesus freed from priests,
Prometheus and his Asia come as one
Spirit to sing at Demogorgon's feasts
Till Harriet's and Mary's pains are done,

He found perhaps that marriage he had dreamed
Among them all—Platonic realms above,
Necessity within the things that seemed,
Substantial shadows hallowed by his love.

Upon the Publication of a First Book of Poems
The Burning Fields, LSU Press, 1991

To see them here brings humbleness, not pride,
Poems so well printed, jacketed, and then
Braced by comments made by generous men
Whose works my own could never stand beside.

Here also is that absence, black despair,
That stared from blank white spaces at my face
Until the courted muse released her grace
And words flowed into verses like a prayer.

Such moments of eternity-in-time
Confirm the Maker in each maker's rhyme.

Warren in Thibodaux
the Southern Literary Festival and Fletcher Lecture Series,
April 1985, Nicholls State University, Thibodaux, Louisiana

You flew down to New Orleans, then drove south
Into a trembling prairie, sea and land
Unstilled by any maker's word or hand
So near the Mississippi's silent mouth.

And there you shared your poems one final time
Unaided though when stage-light beams would blind
Your one unblinded eye you spoke your mind—
"Hopeless! Hopeless!"—yet then read on in rhyme.

Later, at that plantation where you stayed,
Night thickened with your whiskey-tales that strayed
From rooms Jim Bowie owned to where a knife-
Sharp wit cut sheer through dank moth-hours still rife
With bearded oaks that once more made you feel
"After Louisiana nothing seemed real."

Rapture at Twilight
not far from Driskill Hill,
north Louisiana

Far down a winding hillside road
Under the chapel-ground
Where she'd inclined and heard explode
Revival words profound

About the end-times' final night
In which the chosen few
Would be uplifted to the light
While those left got their due,

A woman steers toward Christ alive
As from the town below
Pumped frat-boys in their pickups drive
Toward some snug bungalow.

They've stocked back seats with smokes and beer
And hit sex shops as well
For blow-up dolls they'll hold so dear
When phallic egos swell.

The dolls, tied to the trucks' flat beds,
Float high in twilight skies
Toward which one unsuspecting heads
Till wild revival eyes

See unclothed bodies rising free—
The Rapture come at last!—
And so she slows ecstatically
Up-gazing at The Vast . . .

And finding there a sermon's proof
Above her thrilling sighs
She stops, disrobes, and on the roof
Raises her arms and cries,

And when the wafting rapt-dolls pass
She leaps, then falls pell-mell
Back on her cracking tailbone ass
Waving the saved farewell.

Janitor
< Lt. *janitor,* doorkeeper >
Nicholls State University, Thibodaux, Louisiana

for the custodians

I work these rooms before and after class,
Picking up dusty *Cliffs Notes,* pencils, gum
From this tough stage where boredom spiked with sass
Grew quiet at tragic wisdom's podium.

Most students, like professors, pass before
My busy broom, well-faded shirt, frayed jeans,
My presence what they pay for to ignore,
A lowly ghost of their high ways and means.

They never think how much depends on me,
Blocked water fountains cleared, the scoured johns,
Light bulbs changed out, the heating or A/C
Kept up in this base age of iron and bronze.

And none would dream that I was one of them
Until my father's death made me a man
Who dropped out to become a man like him,
My texts exchanged for bucket, mop, and pan.

Yet in that office-closet where they store
Strong chemicals with implements I use
A long shelf holds books left on desk and floor,
Collaterals abandoned to their muse.

And there, through lunch, door closed, I open doors
Unlocked yet shut to all who hesitate
To run with Heathcliff, Cathy on the moors
Or fall with Milton's Satan to his fate.

Such was my education: words and dust
Together in the depths of bone and brain,
Those sweeping strings of straw and verse that must
Be one in some harmonic final strain.

The Courtyard Plum
Nicholls State University, Thibodaux, Louisiana

It stands alone inside stone courtyard walls
Of this small southern college, close confined
By generator, bench, and all that falls
From cloud or sun or rises from the mind.

The tree moves through its seasons with a grace
That comes of being grafted, pruned, and bred
In China, then Japan, and now a place
Exotic on its semitropic bed:

White umbel clusters opening in snow,
Petals of February's winter-spring
Dropping before bronze leaves break green and slow
And yellow fruit turns blue in ripening

From May until July beside the halls
Where young bards trying haiku pluck a plum,
The season-word for which each haiku calls,
Its images deep hints that quietly come.

And there amid the bending mellow boughs
Still reaching down from Eden creatures feed—
Bumble- and honeybees, jay birds in rows—
Together in the weather of their need

With lizards, crickets, squirrels, and dragonflies
All drawn to feast on craving's bleak predation
And on the tree of life that bears and sighs,
By silence weighed, dying in creation.

The plum tree spreads its branches, roots, and leaves
Just like that tongue in which its petals sing
High psalms of heaven's courts no one perceives
But shapers when their balmy rhymings ring

In praise of manner, port, demeanor, air
By which the plum declares itself a liege
Caught up in this fraught world once whole and fair,
Made better by its bred noblesse oblige.

Before and After Reading
New Orleans, February 2003

in memory of Leo Luke Marcello, 1945–2005

We sat there as an early evening fell
That winter on the old St. Charles Hotel,
Sipping dark coffee, polishing a line,
Community in grounds and sounds ground fine
For rarest listeners, those local rolls
Of Christian scholars, critics, poets, souls.
It wasn't always thus. We knew the tale
Of readings where smart smirks and sighs assail
Verse fleshed with images that bear the Word,
Staves staving off the utterly absurd,
Shunned by some smug editors unannoyed
By changes tolling into a tongueless void.

But not tonight. And so we took our place
Behind the podium-pulpit, sacred space
For poet-rectors, humble yet ordained
To lift up all they hoped their work sustained.
And when you read your elegy for John,
Our brother maker lost to AIDS, then one
About your priest-friend, near here beaten dead
By those young men he prayed for as he bled,
Your smile and twinkling teardrop eyes would shine
As ever in this comedy divine
Where souls untold will hear your poem-bells, pealing,
Say Christ made even death itself a healing.

The Fairfield Gnomes
Fairfield is an elementary school in Shreveport, Louisiana

They grace the Gothic archway to the school
As they have done for more than sixty years,
Those gnomes of education's constant R's,
All numbers, letters, words, and their close kin
In axiom and syntax—diagrams
Of grammars where the mind can know the world
And know itself through radiant translations
Of sentence and equation's golden codes.

The Gnome of Writing prints his alphabet
Raised up by marble pen from marble page,
The building blocks' block capitals that spell
Synonymous tautologies of God,
The Logos' *fiat lux* and *finis est,*
His squinted eyes, cramped fingers, drawn-back face
Grotesques of body's discipline by mind.
And opposite, Arithmetic's balked Elf
Fixing his dumb attention on a row
Of numbers half-abstracted from the slab,
Treasures of weight and measure and degree,
Latent gradations, quiet hierarchies,
A Ptolemaic cosmos after all,
The music of the atom and its spheres.
Then, last, above the ciphers, ABCs,
The Gnome of Reading, given to his book,
A creature's stirred alertness to intent,
Each person, mood, case, number, voice, and tense
A trace of One indwelling yet alone,
His page of thought and nature caught in stone.

Such elements exposed to rain and sun
Still grace the Gothic archway to the school
As they have done for more than sixty years
Guarded by dwarfs transfigured into giants
Whose minds forever strain by earthen light
Dug from the mother veins of brain and ore
To parse and tally, point, and reckon sums
Till number, letter, word, and world are one.

Daddy
Shreveport and Thibodaux

after Sylvia Plath, author of "Daddy"

Some afternoons I waken from a dream
To dream on to the rocker's to-and-fro
And the tick-tock pendulum of a clock
That holds me for a moment out of time
Till long lost scenes come welling from the depths
By happy access in creation's play.
And one such afternoon when winter chill
Brought stillness to each autumn leaf and blade
Stiffened by winds that dry their dew to frost
I saw you making clay pots in your shop.

It took you all your life to reach that place,
The eldest of five brothers and at times
A stand-in father even as a child
Who if you swung your bat and got a hit
Would have to let another run for you
So you could hurry back to baby boys
Card-playing parents left in your sole charge.
On Fridays you would skate down Egan Street
Then over rippling hill bluffs toward the Red
And back again, library books in hand.

At home, in a rocking chair, you'd sit and read
Those books in stacks each weekend, left to right
The piles of read and unread up and down
Till Sundays when you skated back to town,
Your father baffled by his egghead son.
Then after graduation you would work
Some months in Faulkner's world, your weekends spent
Shooting pool in New Orleans till the draft
Found you at last and you became a cook
On Asian ships till A-bombs brought you home.

And there, although the West still drew your blood
(Cooled by a mother's clutching reluctance),
By grace at Highland Baptist Church you met
Saline's Miss Anne, small-town nobility,
Who loved you for yourself, helping you evade
Maternal suffocation just enough

To be the artist you were meant to be
After those long tough teaching days at school
Or summers as a lifeguard at the pool
That kept a wife and child from poverty.

And as your youth gave way to middle age,
A principal at Judson you opposed
The peewee football dads and sanctioned games
In which they all could play, both girls and boys,
And with that stubborn hand-pressed ribbon machine
Cut even eighth-place ribbons so no child
Who tried at all would lack some accolade.
Coach, umpire, fan for soccer, softball, track,
You found that childhood you had been denied
With children whose respect grew into love.

Each year, guided by you, a sixth-grade class
Made murals for the cafeteria wall,
Our New-World story told in grout and tile,
Columbus, Indians, Pilgrims, soldiers massed
In clashing blue and gray, a settled West,
And then this century from Kitty Hawk
To Cape Canaveral, pictures no doubt
Too innocent yet made for innocence,
Each panel immovable, fastened tight
By hidden bolts still known to you alone.

Years later, drained by central-office stress,
Administrative politics, decrees,
At fifty-six you gave up and retired,
Taught college art at Centenary two sweet years
And ran your boyhood's bases when you won
10Ks and marathons till Parkinson's
Slowed you to a shuffle, walker, chair
Whose wheels your weakened fingers clutched and pushed,
Great-hearted racer who pressed on and on
Toward death's black tape broken with your last breath.

And now a decade later I still see
So clear in heightened musings, deepest dreams,
Two images of you: one near the end,
Painting in your wheelchair, stiffened hands
Then capable only of dabs and streaks
That filled a tautened canvas primed in white
With colors pure in form and formlessness,
"Trying something new," you wryly said,
Almost like a child learning ABCs,
Your primer's words of yellow, blue, and red;

The other, thirty years ago this fall,
You singing in your workshop, shaping clay
In male and female obelisk and pot,
Then glazing them in colors of the earth,
Late autumn shades of gold, brown, orange, gray
Fired in a backyard kiln you fenced against
Neighbors afraid to feel creation's heat,
Cones melting under kiln gods undisturbed
By matter's agony or by a love
That forged them too, your passion made serene.

Mother among the Graves
Magnolia Baptist Church,
Saline, Louisiana, April 2000

for Anna Sudduth Middleton

So early in the morning we had come
To stand once more before the Sudduth graves,
For four years now, a Middleton's as well,
By spiderwort and spider undisturbed,
His leveled mound as grassy as the rest,
Stone stained by broken shadows, summer rain.

Your parents' stones lie tilted, sunken, worn,
Their birth and death dates, verses, even names
Obscured by climbing grass and fire-ant mounds,
Your only-sibling brother's much the same,
And you, almost eighty, the last one left
Ungathered to the ashes of your kin.

And right beside my father's stone there stands
Another stone, put up to save a place
In the crowded ground, bearing your own name
And birth date but as yet no Bible verse
Or that last date whose chiseling-in I dread
When you too come to rest among the dead.

But now, though so much given to the past
That waits beyond what time there's yet to be,
You smile and turn in fortitude toward me
To live on as a mother till the end,
Grandmother to your one grandchild whose name
And spirit are your own: Anna Marie.

And as we close the rusted graveyard gates
On plots where our own plots will one day be,
We gaze on pines made radiant at dawn
And on that tree the years have nurtured here,
An old magnolia whose broad leaves at noon
Cover the graves with deep unbroken shade.

Deep Country Epitaph

Here lies untouched by sun or snow
The flesh of one content to go
Out of a place of age and pain
To which she'll not return again.
She rests beside her husband now
Who kept, like her, his wedding vow
Nor thought of any other course—
Neglect, adultery, divorce.
Standards upheld without complaint—
Denial, duty, self-restraint—
She needlepointed that first fall,
The Ten Commandments on the wall.
Six decades took her through each state
That plighted troths enumerate,
The bumper crops, the barren land,
The strong and then the trembling hand,
Rare days she wondered at her choice,
Those fertile nights, the mastering voice,
Nine sons and daughters whom she saw
Become themselves by natural law;
Debilitation, fading, death,
Her husband's last faint kiss and breath,
Long years there living on alone,
Spring cleanings of his house and stone,
Tending blue stars and marigolds
By Mary's rose the dawn unfolds.
Such sacraments of sky and flower
Sustained her in her final hour,
The doctor's, then the pastor's hand
Upon her brow, the funeral planned,
The simple coffin made of pine,
The great King James's *thee* and *thine*,
The nineteenth psalm and twenty-third,
Our Father and St. John's The Word,
Interment near her husband's dust,
And one still doing what he must,
Her eldest son, who, now grown old,
Plants blue star mixed with marigold
In earth that covers the remains

Of one whose love his life contains,
A soul with virtue deep imbued,
Commandment and Beatitude,
Spared late in this most graceless age
That worships its own pride and rage
Modernity's depraved embrace,
Fled far beyond this time, this place.

Two for Life
in Acadie

1. Late February

February 22, 1986

Sleeping alone in a farther room
This morning's mother-to-be
Leaves for now the tragedy
Of ruptured blood and the voided womb.

The husband, nursing coffee, still sits up,
Shocked by the quick miscarriage,
Bitter first fruits of marriage,
Black dregs settled in an empty cup.

He shakes as a grave equation sears
A heart too long in mind's control—
Each lost child: a human soul—
And weeps in quiet his manly tears.

2. Chemo Refused

dying mother to unborn child

I only did what Christ himself would do:
I gave up life to give your life to you.

In Winter Prime

Near Lent the winter deepens toward its noon
When sun-flakes twinkle keen in snow and grass
And stars beyond the stardust of the moon
Pass on within a dark that cannot pass.

Yet even then may come a milder time
When ice sweats cold gold beads that swell and run,
Their melting felt in earth as early prime,
Some subtle fluctuation of the sun.

And in that radiant glade where warm light glows
A yellow dandelion and butterfly
Wake to a false brief spring that comes and goes
Between long afternoons of frosted sky.

Such blooms and wings soon stiffen in the dusk
Of matter's endless winters that still hold
Each fall and spring, each summer's greenest husk,
All caught in plots that plot a tale untold.

Black Lake Tales
Bienville Parish, north Louisiana, 1959

*in memory of my uncle Joseph Lynn Sudduth (1919–1964),
Lt. Colonel, U.S. Army Air Corps*

*Sometimes, though not in wakefulness or sleep
But that strange state just after piercing dreams
When memory traumatically reveals
Objective truths, we find forgotten scenes
Are brought up from the depths like fabled prey
On some taut line, each mythic fish just held
By time's bright hook a moment and then lost
Returning once again, through deeper reeds,
Into those beds no light has ever found.*

They moved through humid blackness toward the shore
Before the dawn disclosed their ghostly forms
Clutching limber poles, damp cans of worms,
A tackle box and rods, and jangling chains.
The forty-year-old uncle and the boy,
His city nephew, ten, an only child
Deep in the summer country of the soul
Soon made their way across a rotted pier
Whose firm planks they remembered yet would test
Until they reached the roped post and the boat.

Unsteadily they stepped from seat to seat,
Rocking the solid bottom with their weight
Until they settled down amid the faint
Black lappings of the little shoreward waves.
They chucked the mud with paddles, pushing off,
And in a quiet no motor would disturb
They pulled and pulled then glided in the trees
Whose shapes and names were clarified by light:
Old water oaks and locusts, tupelos,
Scrub willows, and the sun-drawn cypress stands.

Then drifting near an over-woven grove
The uncle and the nephew baited hooks,
Lowering bobs and sinkers from the poles,

Or from bent rods flicked the shiny spinners
Across the glittering surface of the lake.
And there until the noontide in full bloom
Transformed them with its blazing fragrant rays
Whenever the vibrant line or plunged bob ran
They pulled up from the depths first words reclaimed
As yellow bass, bluegill, and buffalo.

Sometimes the boy would glance aside to find
His uncle fixed intently where a trail
Of water lights sparkled across the dark
In silent rhymes of brightness and the night:
Creation's radiant twinkling in the sheen.
And in such moods the uncle often spoke
Not to the child alone but to the man
The child's ripe innocence barely held within
Of what had long possessed his heart and mind,
Stories gleaned from books and from the book of life.

He said he did not live within the state
But in an unabstracted known domain:
Crests of the buckled uplands, fractured folds
Lifted from the dried primeval seas,
Wrinklings of eons shriveled into hills,
Old salt beds exposed as sour lakes, salines—
Expressions of a depth where nothing grows—
And sandstone ridges, facing inward, steep,
Their sloping backs declining toward the Gulf,
Outcroppings of the logic of the rock.

Such places he had dreamed on Driskill Hill,
Lulled by the undulations of the pines,
Gazing toward far Arcadia and those
Enfolded wolds—Kisatchie, Nacogdoches—
And the great Sabine Uplift under the Red
Where ice floes once brought boulders from the north
To lodge upon the risen inland coast
And where the Raft grew thick to such a reach
That over its rich width from bank to bank
Green willows flowered southward like a stream.

Grappling in bafflement at what he'd heard,
The startled nephew hardly made reply,
Recalling other times his uncle seemed
A voice the spirit uttered from its core,
Speaking of the unspeakable as when
At LSU with Brooks in '41
He studied that same irony he'd feel
Bombing the place from which his fathers came
Till down flak-alley's length he seemed to hear
Cries rising from the Rhine to curse his name.

Later in vital nightmares as he screamed
Fully awake and terrified in sleep,
He flew again beneath a bomber's moon
While all around the skies, like shooting stars,
In molten cockpits fighter pilots fell
Flaming through cindered heavens to the ground.
And yet within those broken smoky clouds
On one most terrible run the dark grew clear
And night's unmeasured beds became Black Lake
Twinkling in winter twilight's brightest stars.

These tales the boy had heard and now again
Saw pain the rugged uncle's sullen face,
A face that once had gazed upon a scene
Come up from unimagined depths of hell:
The death-camps' mangled hills of fetid flesh
Pushed by bulldozers over the lime-pit's edge.
Then, too, like all the world, the uncle lived
Minutes away from total holocaust,
A terror told again when sonic booms
Rolled from targeted Barksdale over the wolds.

And there amid such dreaded recollections,
While baitless lines lay tangled in the weeds,
The uncle found new access to a past
Now called back in full poignancy by grace.
And so he told the boy till latest day
Gave way at last to twilight and the dark
Of what had scarred an unsuspecting heart

When like his nephew he was barely ten,
And as he spoke, his nephew rowed alone,
Listening as his building muscles ached.

The uncle was a boy in '29
Though little of The Crash had touched those hills
Whose poor stayed poor on grim subsistence farms
That yielded corn and greens and black-eyed peas
To brutal toil and hunger's constant pain.
And here within a triple history
Of nature, Holy Writ, and humankind
He knew he had been made from Adam's clay
Dug from the salt-domed valley of the Red,
A place the Rebels held until the end.

The things themselves, familiars of their names,
He saw as science and Genesis and sense:
Creek water pure and cold from leeched gray clays,
The cottonwood, crab apple, sassafras,
The purple morning glory, goldenrod,
The black-eyed Susans, cattails, chinquapins,
Loblolly bogs where rare white arums thrive,
Celestial lilies, star grass, spiderwort—
Such uttered substance once had been a speech,
A rhetoric made tremulous with love.

It was the only world the uncle knew,
And there he roamed alone through Eden's trees
Or with his dog, a young mixed-breed named Will.
At times they ran with dancing, lost in joy,
The dog and master chasing each in turn
Across the ripening watermelon fields
Covered with prickly nettle, stickers, ticks
And fire ants' built-up hills that just fell in
When Will pranced through their nations till he sank
Chest-deep in the crumbled tunnels, stunned and stung.

One late spring day adventure led them on
Farther into the woods than ever before
Beside old dogtrots claimed by rot and vines

And past the deadened fields of girdled trees—
Now glades with brambleberries overgrown—
Then farther still, beyond those hidden rows
Where Indians once grew maize from virgin loam
Until they reached a place whose given name
Had lived in tales kin told as though a myth,
Two hills in massive collapse: The Big Ditch.

The uncle and his dog drew near the ledge
Gingerly peering straight down sixty feet
Into a dense entanglement that came
Climbing up out of chaos into light:
Black alder, sugar maple, oak, and ash,
Magnolias lifting blossoms toward the sun,
And dandelions so golden on a rim
Filled with the noise of crickets that would brush
The silence of the yellow butterflies,
Their mundane strains the music of the spheres.

And standing in a trance upon the brink
The uncle saw his dog a moment late
First leaning toward a hare that hopped below,
Then trying to backtrack from a sliding edge
Of bitterweed and honeysuckle vines
Where he yelped and fell into the undergrowth
From which repeated whimpers pierced by howls
Scared one who stayed till nightfall looking down
Where soon the autumn's galaxy of asters
Would rise in pitiless beauty toward the stars.

Thus caught between pure terror and pure love,
The uncle hesitated and then fled
Running by panicked instinct through the woods,
Lashed by the bramble-briars and nameless dread.
And when at last bounding onto the porch
Breathlessly babbling he hardly knew what
In a house as quiet as midnight on the lake
He roused his father who would take him back
Into the deepened evening, with flashlights,
Lengths of rope, and a downsized .22.

They made their way by impulse, faith, and fate
Back to the ditch in thickest midmost woods,
But then restrained elation was displaced
By instant fear when not one howl was heard
Or whimper as they whistled, called, and cried.
Instead, far down below, a bobcat moved
Eluding the long beams, and, over the brink
From which the dog had fallen there arose
A great horned owl in almost silent flight,
Its hard pinched talons dripping bits of meat.

The father turned his son away in tears
Just as that son as uncle now would turn
From tales recalling things forever lost
Toward paddling to the shore and driving home
While stars and fireflies mingled in the trees.
And when at last the uncle and the boy
Had scraped and gutted the fish, sitting outside
They gazed awhile, in silence and the night,
On old unsounded depths of earth and sky,
Black lakes whose beds no light has ever found.

Flies and Grounders
Jonesboro, Louisiana, 1963

for my cousin, Gordon Sudduth,
Southern Baptist pastor

We played on that grass lot beside your house
All afternoon through long green Easter springs,
The shortleaf pines marking off unmarked lines
With plated bark and wind-swung oblong cones.
And there, where silent heads of clover tolled
In gusts that brushed the latest April blades
So tender now, so hard in summer light,
We came with simple gear—bat, ball, and glove
Well spat on, worn, laced, oiled, and broken in—
And took up our positions on the field.

The game was flies and grounders—one to hit,
The other to snatch, scoop up, or body-block
Till three caught in the air or seven stopped
Dead cold on earth switched out the one-man teams.
Up first, I chocked, spun, bunted, popped up balls
That you knee-skidded, leapt, or dove to clutch
Before they rolled on past you and away
Over the lane toward moldy, sunken woods.

And as you vanished into that dank dark
Stumbling to chase a seventh grounder down
I saw your father's bomber on its run
From England to the Rhine and back again
Past swinging batteries, banked fighter planes,
And acrid flak that even then in sleep
In that front room so close to where we played
Could blind him like black fire in flashback dreams
In one of which a year hence he would die,
Gliding aflame toward night on smoking wings
To join at last lost buddies in the waves
Crashing below chalk cliffs that called them home.
But for a while nightmares let him be,
Next to his bedside window in a chair
Watching you, like a plane, return to base,
Mission fulfilled, an errant grounder found,
The stained ball raised triumphant your glove.

And now, four decades later, on a cane,
Though only fifty, lungs and bone and brain
Infested by those toxic molds that spread
Throughout a church whose souls you've served so well,
You, like your father, pass through flak and flame—
A homeless congregation, some who've left
One who, though ill, did not abandon them,
Delayed insurance settlements, huge bills,
Unsteady mind and body, and your own
Wild flashback dreams to innocence and health—
Your bearing graced by faith and fortitude,
Still fielding flies and grounders in a glove
Yet one not made of leather, oiled and laced,
But magnanimity and guts and love.

In the Bleak Midwinter
Christmas and St. Stephen's Day

Angels and archangels may have gathered there . . .
—*Christina Rossetti*

to my daughter, Anna, at eleven, to read
years hence when the times
of faithful doubting come

Staying up late to play
Once more on Christmas Eve
The role of Santa Claus
For one who would believe
(Though doubt now gives her pause)
In reindeer and the sleigh,

The toyshop gifts, the bells,
St. Nick in white and red,
The elves, the ho-ho-ho's
All dreamed while snug in bed,
Tucked in for years by those
Strong hands where safety dwells,

I know the glittering veil
Of fairy tale and myth
As literal and living
Must be stripped to its pith:
Spirit of Christmas giving,
Love's light that ought not fail.

But then when midnight nears,
My job as Santa done,
I gaze up at the crèche,
The Mother and the Son,
Where myth and history mesh
Or so it now appears.

Yet what if this tableau
Of God's redeeming love—
The Wise Men and the beasts,
The great Star poised above

The shepherds' hillside feasts
With angels in the snow—

Were nothing but a dream,
The deep heart's deepest cry,
Fulfilling fantasy
That though we all must die
We never cease to be
As soul and mind would deem.

So might this story told
Of such a human gift—
Bright fictive mystery!—
Still leave us set adrift
In St. Nick's history,
This bleak midwinter cold.

"If I should die before I wake"
Of a Daughter Who Died at the Age of Ten

for David Mills

So many nights I sat beside your bed
Tucking you in and brushing back your hair
When "Now I lay me down" and books we read
Could bring the sleep of fairy tale and prayer.

And though you seemed untroubled I would say
Before your droopy eyelids closed for good
That if some fear had built up from the day
To tell me and I'd quell it if I could.

And once when winter's early darkness fell
On Dolly's twisted leg and rolled-back eye
Awry from tightest hugs old frights compel
You asked me "Daddy, am I going to die?"

Then pressing both your hands in one warm palm
As I had done the morning of your birth
I told the truth in terms that left you calm
With dreams of many years on mother earth.

Yet now in this dread antiseptic place
By monitors that measure my despair
Too soon I stroke these teardrops from your face
And brush a head strong medicines make bare.

Meanwhile in flesh I know so chastely well
My drawn blood and your own flow vein by vein
In wars between each pale and crimson cell,
Our long defeat's slow holocaust of pain.

And from such pain in frightened eyes that scan
The face of one whose strength was ever there
To soothe you when some fevered dream began
I see a fear grown far too deep to share:

A fear that stays awake in aching sleep
Brought on by drugs too weak for this disease
Which will persist through any watch I keep
And love's great rage no grace can yet appease.

And when the night, departing with your breath
A floor below the floor where you were born
Leaves me those things that I must leave to death
I'll hold them till the soul's last threads are torn.

The Latchkey Child
north Louisiana, the late 1990s

1.

He felt within his pocket for a key
That slowly through the school day's set routine
Of study, lunch, and play had settled down
Below soft clicking marbles won at keeps,
A worn buffalo nickel and a knife
Whose ivory handle bore his father's name
Spun to a blur in games of mumblety-peg.
Meanwhile the yellow school bus which had stopped
Now flashed with bright red warning lights and signs
Before a darkened house where no one was.
The driver pulled the stick back and the doors
Swung open on a place long gone to seed
Since that green spring some forty years ago
When mothers by their gates would wait and gaze
Eagerly down the street each afternoon
To welcome home missed children with a kiss,
Sweet brownies, milk, questions about their day,
And supper cooking slowly on the stove.
Yet for a lonely boy this place was home
Or all of home that he had ever known
Since that cold day four Christmases ago
When taking his shaken face in shaking hands
His mother said things never said before
Of which he could remember only one:
His father would not be there anymore.
The boy slid over the seat and grabbed the strap
Of a heavy see-through schoolbag that had passed
Hand-searches and door signs the teachers' bells
All drew him through: "NO GUNS OR DRUGS ALLOWED."
Then stepping down into the shadow-web
Of January's crackling sapless limbs
He passed the gate whose iron pineapple cups
Had rusted through the years of rain and snow.
The house was from the '40s, cheaply sold
By two who raised four happy children there
But then, becoming frail, at last agreed

To all their children's wishes and moved in
With one of them hard chosen from the rest.
A lovely, warm, and lived-in atmosphere
Still lingered in those rooms through which the boy
Soon made his way into a lightless hall
Where on a ledge an answering machine
Gave out a number greater than his age.
He pushed the message-button, then a click
Began a long sad catalogue of sounds
As messages played back from twelve to one,
Voices of men his father never knew,
His mother's last, apologetic, vague.
The one become a zero, he erased
The disembodied presences and turned
Into the empty kitchen to remove
Another frozen dinner from the stack,
And while it warmed inside the microwave—
The processed chicken shaped like chicken legs,
Thin instant mashed potatoes, greasy peas—
He went alone into the family room
And surfed the hundred channels on the set.
Promiscuous soaps and violent cartoons
Flickered by eyes looking for something else,
A moralistic tale in black and white
Of life within a Carolina town—
Warm, humorous, humane, love's faithful way—
The mothering aunt, the sheriff, and the son.
And when the loud commercials' color came
To interrupt the pleasing pastoral scenes
And tiredness of the day and half a life
Brought glazing eyes toward that deep healing sleep
Where all is lost in symbol and desire,
The boy would gaze upon a photograph
Contained in an ornate Victorian frame,
A woman turning toward him with a smile
Out of the world of memory and dream.

2.

Within his mind that place would never change
From what it was before the great divorce,
Those summers happy parents left him there
With one both bride and widow of the land,
Too old to have a care for anything
Except for life remembered in a pipe
Like one her great-grandmother loved to smoke
Long winter nights before the Yankees came.
Then rocking on the porch until the stars
Appeared in constellations of their names,
Like some wise angel versed in perfect rhymes
She told him in the language of the heart
Of things and ways of things a later age
Could only dimly sense in primal signs
Now taken to be less than what they seem.
A virgin woodland's clustered buttercups
Scenting the fountainheads of icy springs,
The baking fields of maize in dry July,
Blue herons heading south through Chesnut Moons,
Midwinter pansies blooming wild in snow—
These were the things dumb wonder made her praise,
The evident perceptions love would know.
Yet from that realm where word and thing are one
The boy would wake in tears to some blurred world
Where broken words break hearts and egos breed
Evasions, ambiguities, and lies.
He saw the time displayed upon the face
Of a faceless modern watch whose hands would pass
Unnumbered marks above the open gears,
But in his mind another kind of time
Recalled yet ever-present took him back
To June's starred Arcadie, that country house
Where by a double window as he lay
Under a comforter made before the War
He'd waken to his dream: an antique clock
Whose numbers, etched in silver on its disc,

Were circumscribed by those revolving moons
Bright-eyed in animation—quartered, halved,
And full—and one no more than closing eyes
Black as the mattered night in which it sank.
Beyond, a slower disc bore through the years
Its fine, exact depictions of the signs—
The Argo's Keel, the Centaur, and the Cross—
And after these the fixed stars in ascent
Below the empyrean's blazing arc.
Such stars the boy had witnessed from the porch
Those deep clear nights a dying voice recalled
The two of them to something that sustained
His all-but-broken soul through bitter years—
A father gone, a mother barely there—
Years passed alone in some suspended state
From which he would awaken in good time
To live with other kin in that green place
Where recollective prose and measured verse
A small yet steady readership would buy
Provided him enough for those few needs
Beyond what chickens, pigs, and tended rows
Of string beans, sweet potatoes, peas, and corn
Would yield to sweated knowledge of the laws
That govern all from Seraphim to seed.
And so he gave himself to toil's routine,
A lay monk of the Benedictine kind,
Subsiding in the silence of the rites
Whose counterparts, night's brightest heightened fires,
Were elegiac lights that still declared
Prime things that shared in timelessness and time
As did a rusted antebellum clock
Which, when a frail grandmother passed away,
Would come with her estate to him alone.
And by such time as Gothic numbers ticked
In lucent moons, the zodiac, and stars
Contained by the fiery zone's embracing flames
He measured out his life until its end.
And by instructions left beneath the key
That wound the antique clockworks he was placed

At last beside the matriarch he loved
Under a massive oak the pioneers
Had spared from those first woods to shade their graves.
And there, in twinkling leaves, the summer stars
Intense as on the evening when he died
Still warm the night whose doming spheres contain
In lordly ordination, names proclaimed
As brimming emblems shaped by One above
To grace a clock whose winding key is love.

Home

> It is a kind of total grandeur at the end.
> —Wallace Stevens, "To an Old Philosopher in Rome"

> I am going to the inevitable.
> —Philip Larkin, near death

Late middle age, late autumn when a sense
Of ending heightens all we see and are—
The crimson maple leaves now down and dense,
Cane-stubble flames that flicker in the char.

Inside, a clock tocks out the times that rhyme
With measures poets set against a dark
Which brings each season deep into a mime
Of silence where the world grows bleak and stark.

The house for now displays its old décor,
Familiars of the candle and the stars,
Pale rays at twilight fading on the door,
Hearth's ember-ash, the zodiac's marked cars,

The memory with its notches, halls, and nooks,
Scratched records on the antique gramophone,
The keepsakes and the heirlooms and the books,
Those walls of verse from Homer's to our own.

And there we watch again the last gold glow
That far in autumn falls on everything
In turnings of our lives and lines that go
Toward one great end that all beginnings sing:

This mystery of the house in which we dwell,
These cradling graves of starlight and the loam,
These seeds of earth that flower in heaven's dell,
Love's valley where we pass toward love's first home.

The Farmer's Almanac
"for planters, farmers, workers, gentle folk"

Its cover graced by fine antique designs
Year after year printed from those same plates
Whose long-dead craftsmen grasped the things they fixed
In etchings pressed so deep on each inked page—
Black edges splashed by dissipating waves,
Four cornered winds blowing the ghostly foam
Of matter's atoms splattered in salt and air,
And spreading in the center, yielding fields,
Wet furrows urged by patriarchal rays
While farmers plow beneath a smiling sun—
Such pictures bear fair witness to a time
When heart and mind could know the world as one.

And though three hundred years have brought us far
From Harris and those first plain almanacs
Of astral tabulations made for souls
Who crossed the sea and earth by plotted stars,
They still contain what we have never ceased
To yearn for in the long divided nights
Of reason and the fancy's fatal sways—
The news of what's too precious to be news,
Perennial predictions, natural laws,
The times to fish and plant and watch for rain,
Tables of weights and measures, zodiacs
Whose houses match the likened plighted signs
Of heaven and the body, zone by zone.

These brazen correlations well aligned
The later almanacs would decorate
With properties of curatives and lures,
Remedies mixed where faith and science combine—
Foxglove for palpitations, burdock's surge,
Skin glowing with aloe vera, bladderwrack
In thinning and those bilberry brightened eyes,
Mullein for easy breaths, garlic to open
Arteries, cayenne for circulation—
And near these rendered simples long dispensed
By pastoral physicians, happy ads
For weather-sticks bending in ice and sun,

An eight ball's love prognostics, sexy shots
Of would-be virgin brides from Singapore,
And all those notions, lotions, potions, sprays
For bumper crops of greenbacks, beans, and hairs,
Flat muscled bellies rippling, stirring bowels,
And prostates raising cocks up from the dead—
Snake oil of the medicine show Asclepians!

Yet why if now we've come so far beyond
Old pictures of the heavens and the flesh
And tall-tale claims the almanacs still run
Do we keep faith and heed them when we have
The Weather Channel, *Playboy*, CNN,
E-mail, the Internet, and Fax machines,
The Hubble Telescope, the AMA,
Wall Street and Wal-Mart drugs, and A&Ps?
Perhaps, as the cover says, for "the great
And little secrets of the world, visions,
Divinations, nostalgia, curious lore"
Not only in the nostrums and the charts
Of solstice, syzygy, and equinox,
But in the long-dead etchers' finest lines—
Ripe apple orchards russet in the dusk,
A Bible verse cut deep on family stones
By names that stay through centuries the same,
Sealed jars of golden peaches on a shelf
Put up against a window filled with snow,
And most of all in noonday harvest fields
When hay wains pause amid the windy rows
Of hissing ricks that lift the drivers' songs
Till music breaks in silence toward the light
And parted fact and fiction blend as one
In metrical conversions of the heart,
Transcendent transpositions never done
While farmers plow beneath a smiling sun.

The Sniper
Last Report from a Louisianian in Lee's Tigers
northern Virginia, winter, 1864–1865, and after

When snowflakes gray with twilight and the smoke
Of Yankee guns now south of Petersburg
Fall quickly in a windless winter night
Blurring my huddled body crouched so still
Behind this virgin oak's half-blasted trunk,
I think on that warm spring of '61
When Ruffin pulled a lanyard and the shells
Screamed over Charleston harbor toward the fort—
A wild high rhetoric of iron and fire
That set a course to further Lincoln's end
And draw us off a thousand freehold farms.

And with our cows too tense to give their milk
When cannonades disturbed their primal sleep
I joined a corps that Stonewall Jackson drove
Across the Shenandoah at a gallop,
Read Presbyterian tracts, then knelt in prayer
Before shocked Yanks were turned and in detail
Routed again by hard sidehammer blows.
But when in that dark reconnoitering
Jackson was shot by his own jittery men
And one chance death then turned the flank of war
I left my hard-earned colonelcy to try
To be that cause by which the Cause would trace
Its pure effect in one all-telling shell
Like God's creation triggered by his will.

And so for eighteen months I blended in
With summer grass or muddy winter snow,
By silence and my stillness camouflaged
As much as by my worn uncolored clothes,
Discerning through a telescopic sight
Insignia, weapons, banners, officers—
Patches of acorns, diamonds, moons, and shields,
A captain's bars, a major's oak-leaf gold,
A general's triple blue-field silver stars,
My counterpart sharpshooters who all feared
My Whitworth, accurate beyond belief,
And those defining traits I knew so well

From newspaper sketches, stories, and reports
Of "Private" Grant's cigars and Custer's curls—
Heraldic signs I'd shatter with a crack
So that our own St. Andrew's Stars and Bars
Might flutter from the White House and the Dome.

And in those grim extended intervals
Between each precious bullet hoarded well
I thought of all my role and mission meant—
Precision, patience, causes and effects
Of almost infinite complexity,
Archimedes' lever, Zeno's paradox
Converging in intention's mystic act—
And wondered whether I would be the one
To squeeze the trigger till its clicking hurled
Fate's lead upon its set trajectory
High arcing from the muzzle to the blood
In some great death to balance Stonewall's own.
And so in that last winter of the war
I picked off careless officers and sent
A whizzing Minié ball past the slouched hat
Phil Sheridan had flourished as he burned
The furrowed Shenandoah farm by farm
Torching the tall dry stalks of summer corn
Whose scarecrows' tattered butternut and gray
Blazed heavenward, then shriveled in the flames.

Toughened thus by battle I lived to dread
What grandsons witnessed in extreme old age—
Destroyers built at Newport News to dwarf
The *Merrimack,* Richmond a Tredegar
Whose iron has been transformed and magnified,
The sprawl of car-choked highways, shopping malls,
Smog drifting through the Wilderness toward those
Stark nuclear reactors whose dark power
Compels the natives and late immigrants
Who made the mid-Atlantic of our South.
Such technocrats, the planters of their day
With cash-crop data mansions spread across

The Blue Ridge to the fall line and the coast,
Can never now redeem a chattel-mind
That finds the North and South a single thing.

Yet when my memories surface in the souls
Who bear my name and nature we still gaze
On red men who brought corn in "starving time,"
The lone word, *Croatoan,* on a post,
Small farms of ripened peaches, wheat, and oats,
And one young king who came to be a king
With that last word "Remember!" in his heart
As it had been upon his father's tongue
When his stark martyrdom for church and throne
Drew outrage from the New World Cavaliers
Whose heirs would see another Charles declare
Their company's seal be painted on his shield
Not as some mere possession of the realm
But that same Old Dominion which lives on
In steepled villages and freehold fields,
The better dream of Lee and Jefferson.

Song of the Overseer
Louisiana, the 1920s

> The whole assembly of the congregation of Israel shall kill their lambs at twilight.
> —*Exodus 12:6*

I sat there on an easy swayback-mare,
My shotgun, pistol, bullwhip by my side,
Watcher of those brown hands well trained to tear
White bolls from stems that blackened while they died.

No bondsmen then but tenants holding on,
In debt to those who paid them day by day
By sack and weight, some broke in soul and bone,
Time's fugitives who could not run away.

The big house in the distance and the row
Of cabins where each freedman stayed a slave
To keep the planters' sons from plow and hoe
All weathered what their seasons took and gave.

Yet sometimes, plagued by heat in mid-July,
We seemed to be in Pharaoh's stricken land
With loam for bricks but no straw gathered by,
The Mississippi's Lower-Kingdom sand.

And there we toiled between the shack and hall
Till bits drilled deep through earth's sufficient soil
Toward poison-fumes, dead creatures that appall,
The fathers' arpents leased for gas and oil.

Our children will grow gray in that new age
Where factory and plantation are at one
Under no flag that rallies love or rage,
Old Glory and the Stars and Bars undone.

And I, no more the overseer of fields
Where huge mechanic insects grasp and pull
Seeds from seedpods—weevils of their own yields!—
Am pastured now, late autumn's slaughter-bull

While blight spreads wide across the Promised Land
Driving us back to Egypt, mile on mile,
Not plowing forty acres well in hand
But killing lambs at twilight by the Nile.

The Reenactor
upon the centennial reenactment of the Battle of Lafourche Crossing,
fought near the cane fields on Bayou Lafourche outside Thibodaux, Louisiana,
June 20–21, 1863

The day could not have been more like the one
A hundred years ago at this same hour—
Precisely placed, each soldier, horse, and gun—
Even the second day's great thundershower!

And from such fine exactitudes of mind
Came history's images in flesh and blood,
Prophetic elegies at last combined,
The past and present welling in full flood.

Black cannon-smoke pinned down by steady rain
Where Rebels flinched and fell in the riddling lead,
Yankee repeaters firing again, again,
Until time's empty chambers claimed the dead:

These forms deployed within a substance changed—
Authentic blanks instead of hollow shells—
Made ranks to follow namesake ranks that ranged
Over a ground where nothing ever dwells.

And though I know our reenactment's not
Enmeshed in time's iron fabric just the same
As history blind to what time hasn't got—
Things rooted in a transcendental name—

I nonetheless can sense when mustard-flowers
And sugarcane through vital cycles grow
From chronic sleep below those battle-hours
Where what might be awakens and we know

Edenic blends of endlessness and time
Swept back and forth in one still riverbed
Like war and war's depiction in a mime
Till none can tell the living from the dead.

The Given World

I had not seen your face in thirty years
Until a dream released me once again
To be a child upon that columned porch
Watching you as you walked with limp and cane,
So luminous in day's new-risen mist
That hung between the garden and our house.
I always found you there in late July
Whose suns would brown my skin and leave you soaked
As all day your black muscles moved in work
Through rooms you kept yet never could possess.
And where you went I followed deep in play
Watching the red bandana you'd adjust
On hair whose kinks made rings just like my own,
And when you ran the lemon-scented cloth
Softly over the tables and the chairs
Until the fine-grained oak and walnut shone
You sometimes hummed or murmured low and long
Songs of an ancient people of the law
Who once made Pharaoh's bricks from mud and straw.
Midmorning on the porch you had a rest,
Drinking a tall iced glass of lemon tea
For which by the shady hydrant I would pick
Fresh mint as green and tender as our love
And you, with such a fuss, would give me hugs.
Then in a quiet that settled to a calm
Where reason finds its peace by grace alone
You watched the sun pour heat upon a slope
Whose ripened melons darkened in the light
And heard in distant whisperings of the pines
Archaic strains, creation's common tongue.
In time you rose and took me to the field
And while I held the pail you gathered in
By mundane sacral acts fresh elements—
The purple hulls, snap beans, potatoes, corn—
Then left me with your son to play outside
While you went in to make the midday meal.
His name was Louis Gene, "Blue Jeans" to us,
And jeans were all the two of us had on,

Barefooted and half-naked as we tried,
Where rain had left some pools beneath the swings,
To raise up Camelot from southern soil.
We sank our hands together in the mire,
Our black-and-whiteness swirling into brown
And from such well-mixed substance we would shape
Sludge towers crudely scooped from shallow moats
And then a central citadel we topped
With oak-twig poles and leaf-flags from pecans
And striped grasshopper-guards who kept their watch.
Brothers-in-arms from old Round Table days,
We made up tales of Arthur's plighted knights
Who rode forth side by side, the Celt and Moor,
Against the evil kings of south and north.
And when we tired, the hydrant washed away
Caked mud that casually splattered on the mint
While we stood spellbound by the heady smells
Come from the kitchen window with your song.
The floured chicken frying to a crisp,
Milk gravy browned with drippings in the pan,
Potatoes peeled and boiled, then mashed and mixed
With whole fresh milk and butter to a cream,
Sweet rows of golden kernels on the cobs,
The snap beans steamed with pork chunks, purple hulls—
Such flavors and aromas drew us on
In common hunger peaked by common fare.
Yet once you'd placed the platters and the bowls
Upon our dinner table you withdrew
With Louis to a smaller, farther room
And said a separate grace to our one God.
The table cleared, the dishes washed and dried,
You helped my kin to bed and quiet naps
Those long unairconditioned afternoons
In whose great baking light the world grew still.
And on the screened back porch you had your chair,
A rocker where you nodded off and dozed
Until the others woke and called your name.
Sometimes I sat beside you on the floor

Playing with Minié balls and arrowheads
Dug on our autumn walks from those high banks
Down which the sweet blackberries we would pick
Fruited outside of history in their time.
When older I would fight the Civil War
Lining up Rebs and Yanks beneath your feet,
A hundred painted soldiers blue and gray
Yet of the southern slaves no figurine
Except a picaninny stableboy
Smiling and holding out an iron ring
Toward horsemen in the mansion's Doric shade.
To such flawed reenactments of a dream
In which the Rebels always yelled and won
You uttered nothing, having heard the tales
From great-grandparents who had known them all—
Fire-eaters, carpetbaggers, scalawags,
Knights of the White Camellia, demagogues,
Sadistic overseers, racist Yanks,
And shysters in the Freedmen's Bureau frauds.
And yet I still recall one afternoon
When turning my attention from the War
You told me of a far-off summer day
When playing by the Cane at Grand Ecore
You found in crumbling bluffs of primal clay
Old traces of a Caddoan canoe.
Later the archaeologists who came
From Baton Rouge explained how it was made,
And after, in your being's inmost core,
You dreamed of those who lived here for an age
Before the world of masters and their slaves,
Humans whose skin was neither black nor white,
A native race, at peace with plain and glade.
You saw them burn an oak around the base,
Then push the dark trunk sparkling in the dust
To be scooped out with shells and launched at dawn
Through moonbeam-ripples gleaming in the stream.
Your dream would end when nighttime brought them back,
Those fishermen who worked with hand and spear,

Weighed down by bass and perch for which they sang,
Their paddles swirling starlight on the foam
As though they flowed along the Milky Way
Through chaos and creation toward their home.
But your own world was no such stable place,
Nor those canoes the vessels where in chains
Below the decks your fathers lay enslaved
By evils Appomattox did not end,
Nor did those Sixties when my kin would die
And you and I, so close, would seldom meet
Although at times I wrote and sent you verse
That flowered from a grounded pastoral dream.
For then the two estates that forced the War
Saw all your children victims of the wind—
Sons lost to sprawling cities, gangs or drugs,
And daughters to desertion or divorce,
The slaves, like all of us, to race and sex
In Egypt's bleak new kingdom of the dead.
And in those days, in hospital, alone,
Legless from diabetes, almost blind,
Your husband and your children long since gone,
You cast your mind back forty years or more
To one with whom you'd shared a given world
So far from English elms and tropic palms
Yet rooted in the manor and the clan,
The chieftain and the village, not the town.
And so, in that last season of your life,
Remembering my verses and your dream,
You made a will that gave your land to me—
The cabin, corn patch, garden, sandy road—
That lay beside my dead kin's great estate.
And when astonished lawyers made it known
That you had left the earth itself to one
Who rented out rich fields he'd never turned,
Even that house you kept so long ago,
I felt within the depths of heart and mind
A love no ideology can know.
And standing at the center of our world

Along a grassy path once sand alone,
Grains drifting from my hands in changing winds,
I knew the only thing that I could do.
You had a single child who'd come back south,
Escaped from some dread ghetto of the north,
A youngest son who labored in the mill
Stacking the long sawn boards of yellow pine
That round the lake would stand again in time
When oil-and-gas men built their summer homes.
This son had been included in the will
Inheriting the little you had left
In heirlooms, cash, and goods, but not the land
Unless by that late scribbled codicil
You added when you heard he might return,
Shakily made by a trembling palsied hand
And witnessed by no one save God alone,
Your son would leave the mill and work the soil,
Not only his, but mine, which we would share
As stewards of a place three races claimed.
And when he saw me cross the lumberyard
One dusk as he was quitting for the day
He heard a nickname grown so faint with time—
"Blue Jeans! Blue Jeans!"—that he was slow to turn,
But then his cautious walk became a run,
And we embraced: knights-errant of your love.
That night we slept as brothers on the floor
In your abandoned cabin, side by side,
And in a month, the tenants' lease expired,
Moved in that house where you had cooked and cleaned,
Restoring your old place for guests and kin,
Joint masters of a land we both would serve.
And when the first-year fields lay gleaned and still,
Frosted under a distant autumn sun,
We made our way together to the plots
So far apart, my family's and your own.
And though we had to walk the greater way
To find your woodland resting-place we stayed
In prayer and meditation by your stone

Until a heightened brightness of the sun
Blackened the undersides of deep green leaves
On oaks that slaves had planted as a sign
Of some well-tempered realm of dark and light
Where we live best in exile till we come
From Eden to the New Jerusalem:
That dappled ground beneath each yeoman's trees.

Epiphany in Lent

The last parade has finished in the dusk
And all the floats come back through Thibodaux
From downtown to the college parking lot.
The king and queen and princesses have gone
To dance at fancy balls till midnight brings
This dark night of the liver to its end.
Like witches, ghosts, and trolls at Halloween
Banished on All Saints Day, these costumed gods—
Bacchus, Venus, Mars—now vanish into ash.
The power lines and trees are hung with beads
A few of which will be there in July,
Dry, cracked, and bleached through Caesar's summer reign.
The air still smells of beer and barbecue—
Elements bodies bless at Mardi Gras—
And diehard revelers head to bayou bars
While I, with curtains drawn, remain apart
As I have done for more than forty years
Both from the Protestant north and Catholic south,
Louisiana's European divide:
My '50s Shreveport with its endless Lent
Of guilt and blue laws regnant in between
The red-light streets and "game" ships on the Red
And Thibodaux's high feasts of flesh and blood
Lashed to a passionate abstinence,
Those twin sad aftermaths of Christendom.
And there I stay, secluded with the muse,
Heeding the poet's calling to withdraw
So that he can more fully come to be
The alien celebrator of his home
Shown in the heartfelt psalms his mind refines,
The native foreigner who carries on
As crafter of the wordsmith's mysteries
Forging with fire and sweat his image-beads
Like throws that hang on lines like lines of poems
Or pollen riming spring's Bienville hills,
Fat Tuesday, thin Ash Wednesday, hymned as one.

Parishioners

For Bishop Charles Jenkins and Father John Senette
of the Episcopal Diocese of Louisiana

1. The Wretched Sexton

Divorced and difficult, a grumpy man,
On Saturdays when no one ever came
Except the ladies of the altar guild
Gracing the chancel's ledge with autumn grain,
You worked alone weeding the flower beds,
Cursing the lilies causing all this fuss.
Your wife was Lily, her new husband Gus.

2. The Lay Rector

Dressed in clerical black, his collar white
And high, shirt buttoned up, no tie,
Ascetic, severe, malicious, pale and fey,
A giver of record—advice, the widow's mite—
Though his inheritance had made him quite
Well off, he had a calling, he would say,
To tell new priests, who may have had misgivings,
That they were only curates of his living.

3. Sacrificial Giving: Old Miser Makes a Pledge

Watching my dollars, quarters, dimes
To pledge my share to help repair
Our church, I've switched, though near despair
Jack Daniel's out for Early Times.

4. A Lady of Tradition

Having held with Eliot through change and strife
That "the spirit kills, the letter giveth life"
She wrote in the new prayer book that upset her:
"I'm against all change, even for the better."

5. R.I.P.

Old Harridan lies here most peacefully.
She's in a better place. And so are we.

6. The Yuppie Archdeacon

Determined that youth would never pass me by,
I lived clean till one day, just hitting my stride,
I broke through to the runner's apoplectic high,
Clutched my washboard gut, doubled up, and died.
Go tell my wife, who mourns me in black crepe,
That not all husbands die in such great shape.

7. The New Priest

Looking across the pews on that first day
He thinks of sending out his resumé.
But no. He's tired of moving. And, in time,
Each face will make a sermon or a rhyme.

White Wings
Of Kate Mulvaney, Irish Acadian Traiteur

in memory of James A. Sinclair

As the deer longs for the water-brooks,
So longs my soul for you, O God.
   —*Psalm 42:1*

Louisiana State Museum,
December 15, 1915

   Curator:
I know the kind of deer that trapper brought
For me to see, shot near Lake Maurepas—
Odocoileus virginianus—
A spindly leggèd, short-tailed, hoof-toed beast
Widespread across the state, this one a male,
Its rack of antlers ready to be shed
Now so near to winter, an albino
With rare pink eyes and with two teeth knocked out,
A bullet-furrowed tongue and riddled side,
And something I had never seen before,
Six buds along the spine where feathery hairs
Seemed set to grow and lift toward Seraphim
Or Parnassus an angel-Pegasus,
For this must be a living legend dead,
White Wings, the mythic vicar of the swamp.

December 14, 1915

   Kate Mulvaney:
December's winds leave even cypress iced
In flooded wetlands by Lake Maurepas
Where I have lived in this unpainted shack
Ten years with my mulatto friend, Lebasse,
Concocting cures for asthma, burns, and pains
Of flesh and soul and mind and thankless love.
My potions came from simples of the swamp:
Palmetto, goldenrod, and mistletoe,
White-petaled poison hemlock, gentian,
Red milkweed, elderberry, pennywort,
Hackberry, pumpkin ash, and buttonbush.

And there as well were animals I loved:
White ibises, screech owls, and ruddy ducks,
Red bats and twilight bats, the cotton mouse,
All slinky salamanders, newts, and toads,
The slider turtle, snapping turtle, skinks,
The racer snake and mud snake, moccasins,
The bird-voiced and the gray and box-tree frogs—
Familiars of the witch some thought I was.

But they were wrong. I was a city girl
Whose father once taught Dubliners their Greek
And who, come home from that dark Quarter bar
He tended after some obscure disgrace
Forced him to quit our Ireland's snakeless green
For this green world of snakes and water-fields,
Would read Theocritus till I could hear
Far shepherd pipes that gathered in the sheep
Bleating below the slopes of Helicon.

And then I met him, Irish to the core,
That fair-skinned Daniel Weyman who would drink
So much my father pushed him from his glass
Only for him to sprawl out by my door,
Begging me hard to let him be the one,
A charmer in whose face I'd look and see
Myself reflected—blue-eyed, russet-haired—
His voice a wind that left its seeds in me
Where Celtic roots would flower into love.

Or so I thought. But Dan soon turned morose,
Not drinking now, not doing anything
But reading, smoking, railing at the past,
Damning Atlanta where he'd been disbarred,
Spending his last few thousands, slighting his wife,
Whom (though he'd not divorced her) he called X,
Expecting me to labor, as I did—
From passion, then from pity, then routine.
At first I worked at home as best I could—
Making plain goods of flour and eggs to sell,

Teaching the little rich girls notes and scales,
Then peddling vetiver's sweet Asian root
Or salves and powders drawn from plants I found,
Gathered on wetland walks all summer long
Between lakes Ponchartrain and Maurepas.

Five times evicted over fifteen years,
We parted when he left me for the gold
And diamonds his dead uncle had in mines
In Africa, Australia; then he wed
A nineteen-year-old girl and ran a bank
As I, his "gift" wife, never even "kept,"
Had smallpox while his teenage bride had twins.
And so I found myself at Maurepas,
Talking no more to any but Lebasse,
My fellow-soul, companion, confidant
And to those creatures whose dumb Eden tongue
I understood as none since Adam had:
Swamp rabbits that ate carrots from my lap,
White-striped gray mockingbirds perched in my hand,
Quail preening as I stroked them on my knees,
Squirrels nesting in my ragged stocking-socks.
And though I with my pustule-pitted skin,
Soft snowy hair, claw hands—a drag-foot hag!—
Would seem beyond redemption's loving grace
There came a dying doe that had a fawn
Beside my cabin door—albino, male,
Pink-eyed and deaf, and either side his spine
Six nubbin humps for wings to bring me home
To that Seraphic circle round the throne
Of One who spoke those words that made the world.
I called him White Wings for his wings I dreamed
Would waft me into heaven's meadowlands,
But though he gave me hope that I could fly
Beyond the common burdens of this earth
One day he suffered for and with me here.

It was near mid-December on a road
Between the swamp and lake where I had gone

To gather fruit from holly, mistletoe
For red-and-white high winter Christmas feasts,
When a long black chauffeured car first slowed, then stopped,
And from the backseat lunged an angry Dan.
His younger wife, twin daughters saw me plain
And one girl, scared, cried "Swamp Witch! Swamp Witch! There!"
And Dan, to justify his guilt and fear,
Chased me into the razor grass and yelled
That I had haunted him his whole new life.
But rather than atone for leaving me
He smashed in, with his pistol, my front teeth
Then shot me in the mouth through cheek and tongue,
Pushing me deep into the soggy ground
Beyond the matted blades, though loath to kill
A "witch" whose power, from death, might reach him still.
They drove away and left me there to die,
But soon I felt a breath so soft and cool
Above me and I saw White Wings alight
With two teeth gone, a bullet-plowed blood-mouth,
And bruise-wounds on the same side as my own.

January 6, 1916
Epiphany

Curator:

That much we know—or heard from Kate's Lebasse,
Whom my young helper interviewed at length.
She said that Kate was buried in the swamp
Among those things she spoke both with and of.
Lebasse called him "the white one" and she swore
That late on Christmas Eve their White Wings came
To bear Kate's soul, as his flesh took her flesh,
Through air to hear the hymns of Seraphim,
Those six-winged angels like this six-nubbed back,
This carcass of one dead yet who still lives
Beyond the farthest stars, this mythic fact
That my hard earthbound science cannot explain.

After Katrina
Noah's Raven

Noah . . . sent forth a raven; and it went to and fro
until the waters were dried up from the earth.
   —*Genesis 8:6-7*

[In the new age] Noah was the first tiller of the soil.
   —*Genesis 9:20*

He loosed the window latch
And then he loosened me,
My grim cavort
The first report,
Now made belatedly.

From gopher-wood and thatch
I plied by eye and wing
The ruffled weather,
Wave and feather,
Black froth the sea-winds fling.

Yet there was nothing there
But fountains of the deep
And heaven's wells
Washing great swells
Of salt the drowning weep.

Then hunting everywhere
Below a rounding moon
I felt my screech
Grow Eden-speech
We shared in that long noon

Whose fallen silent leaves
With Adam's clacking bones
Are swept through seas
My singing frees
From brine's dumb undertones.

And though a dove retrieves
From olives on the heights

Her leaf and lands
In Noah's hands
To coo away wild frights

And though she be the high
Meek queen of that new realm
Of peace and love,
The Holy Dove
No flood will overwhelm,

By foaming star tides I
Still fly unsounded ground
That only sweat
Makes fertile yet,
This raven-dark profound.

Hurricane Baby

They lie there in the golden afterglow
Of hurricane and twilight and the slow
Powerless hours through which they'll stay so still
Till air moves cool past each wet windowsill.
Outside spent gales adrift in sweet release
Blow mild by flattened cane until they cease.
Blue herons high in cypress preen and sleep,
Their hours those primal hours all beings keep.
And with the clocks, A/C, and TV dead,
No light for books, they have the dark instead
In which he turns to touch, then kiss her there
Lost in a gentle storm of flesh and hair.

The Fiddler of Driskill Hill

Bienville Parish, north Louisiana;
Driskill Hill: the highest point of elevation in Louisiana

for Ann Gresham, who, as a girl, played on Driskill Hill

Midnight in mid-July I come
Climbing through short-leaf pine
Up Driskill Hill to practice this
Old craft of staff and line.

The weathered greensand top's a stage
On which alone I thrum
These country numbers dark barred owls
Detect in oak and gum.

Below the crest none hear those notes
My bow brings from the strings
For I'm the fiddler of that dance
Where stars go round in rings.

So I slick up my horsehaired stick
With rosin from these trees,
Performing pastoral ballad-psalms
For pines and cypress knees.

I sing of winter winds that rime
The hill's hard ironstone cap
And of a young spring dawn that draws
The prime trunks' rising sap.

I sound deep summer's long green tone
That stays inside my head,
Then sweep harsh strings for fall's dry leaves
Blazed orange, yellow, red.

Sometimes I climb the highest pine
On this our highest hill
As daybreak breezes play through limbs
Where light and silence spill.

I spy the natural gas fields there
Ignited by the sun,

Sweet water filling Sugar Creek
Below Mount Lebanon.

Mount Olive, Jordan Mountain, too,
Are not that far away,
The Bible mapping wilderness
When settlers came to stay.

And though they lie by parish lines
Far north and south unseen,
I praise a name and holy place,
Arcadia, Saline.

And thus atop green Driskill Hill
Each year in high July
I sing what is and ought to be
And will until I die:

For that's what bow and strings are for,
To raise things up in song
Between The Fall and Paradise
And urge the world along.

www.ingramcontent.com/pod-product-compliance
Lightning Source LLC
Chambersburg PA
CBHW022109160426
43198CB00008B/410